HISTORY'S MOST INFLUENTIAL
WOMEN

FROM THE Late 1700s TO THE Late 1800s

Elisabeth Vigée-Lebrun to Florence Nightingale

EDITED BY KATHLEEN KUIPER

Educational Publishing

IN ASSOCIATION WITH

EDUCATIONAL SERVICES

Published in 2024 by Britannica Educational Publishing
(a trademark of Encyclopædia Britannica, Inc.)
in association with Rosen Educational Services, LLC
2544 Clinton Street, Buffalo, NY 14224.

Copyright © 2024 Encyclopædia Britannica, Inc. Britannica, Encyclopædia Britannica, and the Thistle logo are registered trademarks of Encyclopædia Britannica, Inc. All rights reserved.

Rosen Educational Services materials copyright © 2024 Rosen Educational Services, LLC. All rights reserved.

Distributed exclusively by Rosen Educational Services.
For a listing of additional Britannica Educational Publishing titles, call toll free (800) 237-9932.

First Edition

Britannica Educational Publishing
Michael I. Levy: Executive Editor
Marilyn L. Barton: Senior Coordinator, Production Control
Steven Bosco: Director, Editorial Technologies
Lisa S. Braucher: Senior Producer and Data Editor
Yvette Charboneau: Senior Copy Editor
Kathy Nakamura: Manager, Media Acquisition
Kathleen Kuiper: Manager, Arts and Culture

Editor: Kathleen Kuiper
Book design: Michael Flynn

Photo credits: Cover https://commons.wikimedia.org/wiki/File:22-16-154-sacagawea.jpg; p. 8 https://en.wikipedia.org/wiki/File:Mary_Wollstonecraft_by_John_Opie_(c._1797).jpg; p. 32 https://commons.wikimedia.org/wiki/File:The_Bront%C3%AB_Sisters_by_Patrick_Branwell_Bront%C3%AB_restored.jpg; p. 53 https://commons.wikimedia.org/wiki/File:Elizabeth_Cady_Stanton_and_Susan_B._Anthony.jpg; p. 57 https://commons.wikimedia.org/wiki/File:Florence_Nightingale_by_Charles_Staal,_engraved_by_G._H._Mote.jpg.

Cataloging-in-Publication Data

Names: Kuiper, Kathleen.
Title: From the late 1700s to the late 1800s—Elisabeth Vigée-Lebrun to Florence Nightingale / edited by Kathleen Kuiper.
Description: New York : Britannica Educational Publishing, in Association with Rosen Educational Services. 2024. | Series: History's most influential women | Includes glossary and index.
Identifiers: ISBN 9781641900720 (library bound) | ISBN 9781641900713 (pbk) | ISBN 9781641900737 (ebook)
Subjects: LCSH: Women--Biography--Juvenile literature. | Women--History--Juvenile literature.
Classification: LCC HQ1123.K87 2024 | DDC 920.72 B--dc23

Manufactured in the United States of America

CPSIA Compliance Information: Batch #CWBRIT24. For further information contact Rosen Publishing at 1-800-237-9932.

CONTENTS

Introduction. 4
Elisabeth Vigée-Lebrun 6
Mary Wollstonecraft 7
Germaine de Staël 9
Jane Austen 15
Sacagawea 22
Sojourner Truth 25
Dorothea Dix 27
Charlotte and Emily Brontë 29
Victoria 37
Susan B. Anthony and
    Elizabeth Cady Stanton 48
Florence Nightingale 55
Glossary. 62
For More Information 63
Index 64

INTRODUCTION

"Forget conventionalisms; forget what the world thinks of you stepping out of your place; think your best thoughts, speak your best words, work your best works, looking to your own conscience for approval."
— *Susan B. Anthony (1815–1906)*

The world is filled with fascinating women, and each woman has her own compelling story. This book contains profiles of striking individuals who serve as outstanding representatives of their gender. It covers many of the most noteworthy, influential women from around the globe who lived between the late 1700s and the late 1800s.

Most of these women managed to flourish in the face of adversity, and some became powerful rulers. The reign of Queen Victoria I during this time period was one of the longest in history. She ruled the United Kingdom for almost 64 years. So influential was she during her lengthy reign that she has been immortalized by having an epoch named after her—the Victorian Age.

Rather than wield power themselves, some of the individuals featured in this title came to the fore by helping to empower other women. Mary Wollstonecraft wrote a compelling argument for the education of women and their social equality in the late 1700s. In the 1800s, Susan B. Anthony and Elizabeth Cady Stanton struggled to win the right to vote for women in America. After their deaths, their work culminated in the 19th amendment of the United States Constitution in 1920, which granted women this right.

Some women fought for the rights of other marginalized groups. In the 1800s, Sojourner Truth, a former enslaved woman, spoke out against slavery as well as for equal rights for women. Dorothea Dix petitioned for the compassionate care of people with mental illnesses and humane conditions for prisoners.

The medical professionals among the elite individuals featured in this book impacted the masses by not only their service but by advancing the field of health care as well. Florence Nightingale, fondly remembered primarily as a nurse, was also a tireless social reformer who was instrumental in overhauling military medical and purveyance systems. She also devised models for the practice of nursing that are used to this day.

Other women left indelible marks on the world through their creativity. The French artist Elisabeth Vigée-Lebrun painted portraits that captured a moment in time in her own distinctive style. In their novels, writers like Jane Austen and Charlotte and Emily Brontë closely observed life and society in 1800s England while also examining universal truths about human nature. Charlotte Brontë's *Jane Eyre* was an immediate hit with critics and readers when it was first published, while the dramatic and poetic nature of Emily's *Wuthering Heights* wasn't fully appreciated until years later. Regardless, both novels are considered prime examples of superb English literature—as is Austen's entire oeuvre.

The influence of these women, and the others profiled in this book, reverberates throughout the ages. Their leadership has served to enrich, enlighten, and shape modern society. These amazing and influential individuals have given all of us, men and women alike, something to admire and strive for in our own lives.

ELISABETH VIGÉE-LEBRUN

(b. April 16, 1755, Paris, France—d. March 30, 1842, Paris)

The French painter Marie-Louise-Elisabeth Vigée-Lebrun (also spelled LeBrun or Le Brun) was one of the most successful women artists (unusually so for her time) and was particularly noted for her portraits of women.

Her father and first teacher, Louis Vigée, was a noted portraitist who worked chiefly in pastels. In 1776 she married an art dealer, J.B.P. Lebrun. Her great opportunity came in 1779 when she was summoned to Versailles to paint a portrait of Queen Marie-Antoinette. The two women became friends, and in subsequent years Vigée-Lebrun painted more than 20 portraits of Marie-Antoinette in a great variety of poses and costumes. She also painted a great number of self-portraits, in the style of various artists whose work she admired. In 1783, because of her friendship with the queen, Vigée-Lebrun was grudgingly accepted into the Royal Academy.

On the outbreak of the Revolution in 1789, she left France and for 12 years lived abroad, traveling to Rome, Naples, Vienna, Berlin, Saint Petersburg, and Moscow, painting portraits and playing a leading role in society. In 1801, she returned to Paris but, disliking Parisian social life under Napoleon, soon left for London, where she painted portraits of the court and of Lord Byron. Later she went to Switzerland (and painted a portrait of Mme de Staël) and then again (*ca.* 1810) to Paris, where she continued to paint until her death.

Vigée-Lebrun was a woman of much wit and charm, and her memoirs, *Souvenirs de ma vie* (1835–37; "Reminiscences of My Life"; English translation *Memoirs of Madame Vigée Lebrun*), provide a lively account of her life and times. She was one of the most technically fluent portraitists of her era, and her pictures are notable for freshness, charm, and sensitivity of presentation. During her career, according to her own account, she painted 900 pictures, including some 600 portraits and about 200 landscapes.

MARY WOLLSTONECRAFT

(b. April 27, 1759, London, Eng.—d. Sept. 10, 1797, London)

The English writer Mary Wollstonecraft was a passionate advocate of educational and social equality for women.

The daughter of a farmer, Wollstonecraft taught school and worked as a governess, experiences that inspired her views in *Thoughts on the Education of Daughters* (1787). In 1788, she began working as a translator for the London publisher James Johnson, who published several of her works, including the novel *Mary: A Fiction* (1788). Her mature work on a woman's place in society is *A Vindication of the Rights of Woman* (1792), which calls for women and men to be educated equally.

In 1792, Wollstonecraft left England to observe the French Revolution in Paris, where she lived with an American, Captain Gilbert Imlay. In the spring of 1794, she gave birth to a daughter, Fanny. The following year, distraught over the breakdown of her relationship with Imlay, she attempted suicide.

Wollstonecraft returned to London to work again for Johnson and joined the influential radical group that gathered at his home, which included William Godwin, Thomas Paine, Thomas Holcroft, William Blake, and, after 1793, William Wordsworth. In 1796, she began a liaison with Godwin, and on March 29, 1797, Mary being pregnant, they were married. The marriage was happy but brief; Mary Wollstonecraft Godwin died 11 days after the birth of her second daughter, Mary. (This daughter would

FROM THE LATE 1700S TO THE LATE 1800S
ELISABETH VIGÉE-LEBRUN TO FLORENCE NIGHTINGALE

later marry Percy Bysshe Shelley and write *Frankenstein; or, The Modern Prometheus*, one of the great Romantic novels of the time.)

Wollstonecraft's *A Vindication of the Rights of Woman* is one of the trailblazing works of feminism. Published in 1792, it argued that the educational system of her time deliberately trained women to be frivolous and incapable. She posited that an educational system that allowed girls the same advantages as boys would result in women who would be not only exceptional wives and mothers but also

Mary Wollstonecraft's A Vindication of the Rights of Woman *created quite a stir in its day, fueling the fight for women's rights and inspiring feminists everywhere.*

capable workers in many professions. Other early feminists had made similar pleas for improved education for women, but Wollstonecraft's work was unique in suggesting that the betterment of women's status be effected through such political change as the radical reform of national educational systems. Such change, she concluded, would benefit all society.

The publication of *Vindication* caused considerable controversy but failed to bring about any immediate reforms. From the 1840s, however, members of the incipient American and European women's movements resurrected some of the book's principles. It was a particular influence on American women's rights pioneers such as Elizabeth Cady Stanton and Margaret Fuller.

The life of Mary Wollstonecraft has been the subject of several biographies, beginning with her husband's *Memoirs of the Author of A Vindication of the Rights of Woman* (1798, reissued 2001, in an edition edited by Pamela Clemit and Gina Luria Walker). Those written in the 19th century tended to emphasize the scandalous aspects of her life and not her work. With the renewed interest in women's rights in the later 20th century, she again became the subject of several books. *The Collected Letters of Mary Wollstonecraft*, assembled by Janet Todd, was published in 2003.

GERMAINE DE STAËL

(b. April 22, 1766, Paris, France—d. July 14, 1817, Paris)

Germaine de Staël, the French-Swiss woman of letters, political propagandist, and conversationalist, epitomized the European culture of her time, bridging the history of ideas from Neoclassicism to Romanticism. As Madame de Staël, she also gained fame by maintaining a salon for leading intellectuals. Her writings include novels, plays, moral and political essays, literary criticism, history, autobiographical memoirs, and even a number of poems. Her most important literary contribution was as a theorist of Romanticism.

EARLY LIFE AND FAMILY

She was born Anne-Louise-Germaine Necker, the daughter of Swiss parents, in Paris. Her father was Jacques Necker, the Genevan banker who became finance minister to King Louis XVI. Her mother, Suzanne Curchod, the daughter of a French-Swiss pastor, assisted her husband's career by establishing a brilliant literary and political salon in Paris.

The young Germaine Necker early gained a reputation for lively wit, if not for beauty. While still a child, she was to be seen in her mother's salon, listening to, and even taking part in, the conversation with that lively intellectual curiosity that was to remain her most attractive quality. When she was 16, her marriage began to be considered. William Pitt the Younger was regarded as a possible husband, but she disliked the idea of living in England. She was married in 1786 to the Swedish ambassador in Paris, Baron Erik de Staël-Holstein. It was a marriage of convenience and ended in 1797 in formal separation. There were, however, three children: Auguste (b. 1790), who edited his mother's complete works; Albert (b. 1792); and Albertine (b. 1796), who was allegedly fathered by Benjamin Constant.

POLITICAL VIEWS

Before she was 21, Germaine de Staël had written a romantic drama, *Sophie, ou les sentiments secrets* (1786), and a tragedy inspired by Nicholas Rowe, *Jane Gray* (1790). But it was her *Lettres sur les ouvrages et le caractère de J.-J. Rousseau* (1788; *Letters on the Works and the Character of J.-J. Rousseau*) that made her known. There is in her thought an unusual and irreconcilable mixture of Rousseau's enthusiasm and Montesquieu's rationalism. Under the influence of her father, an admirer of Montesquieu, she adopted political views based on the English parliamentary monarchy. Favoring the French Revolution, she acquired a reputation for Jacobinism. Under the Convention, the elected body that abolished the monarchy, the moderate Girondin faction corresponded best to her ideas.

Protected by her husband's diplomatic status, she was in no danger in Paris until 1793, when she retreated to Coppet, Switzerland, the family residence near Geneva. It was here that she gained fame by establishing a meeting place for some of the leading intellectuals of western Europe. Since 1789, she had been the mistress of Louis de Narbonne, one of Louis XVI's last ministers. He took refuge in England in 1792, where she joined him in 1793. She stayed at Juniper Hall, near Mickleham in Surrey, a mansion that had been rented since 1792 by French émigrés. There she met Fanny Burney (later Mme d'Arblay), but their friendship was cut short because Mme de Staël's politics and morals were considered undesirable by good society in England.

She returned to France, via Coppet, at the end of the Terror in 1794. A brilliant period of her career then began. Her salon flourished, and she published several political and literary essays, notably *De l'influence des passions sur le bonheur des individus et des nations* (1796; *A Treatise on the Influence of the Passions upon the Happiness of Individuals and of Nations*), which became one of the important documents of European Romanticism. She began to study the new ideas that were being developed particularly in Germany. She read the elderly Swiss critic Karl Viktor von Bonstetten; the German philologist Wilhelm von Humboldt; and, above all, the brothers August Wilhelm and Friedrich von Schlegel, who were among the most influential German Romanticists.

But it was her new lover, Benjamin Constant, the author and politician, who influenced her most directly in favor of German culture. Her fluctuating liaison with Constant started in 1794 and lasted 14 years, although after 1806 her affections found little response.

LITERARY THEORIES

At about the beginning of 1800, the literary and political character of Mme de Staël's thought became defined. Her literary importance emerged in *De la littérature considérée dans ses rapports avec les institutions sociales* (1800; *A Treatise of Ancient and Modern Literature* and *The Influence of Literature upon Society*). This complex work, though not perfect, is rich in new ideas and new perspectives—new, at least to France. The fundamental theory, which was to be restated and developed in the positivism of Hippolyte Taine, is that a work must express the moral and historical reality, the zeitgeist, of the nation in which it is conceived. She also maintained that the Nordic and classical ideals were basically opposed and supported the Nordic, although her personal taste remained strongly classical. Her two novels, *Delphine* (1802) and *Corinne* (1807), to some extent illustrate her literary theories, the former work being strongly sociological in outlook, while the latter work shows the clash between Nordic and southern European mentalities.

BANISHMENT FROM PARIS

She was also an important political figure and was regarded by contemporary Europe as the personal enemy of Napoleon. With Constant and his friends she formed the nucleus of a liberal resistance that so embarrassed Napoleon that in 1803 he had her banished to a distance of 40 miles (64 km) from Paris. Thenceforward, Coppet was her headquarters, and in 1804 she began what she called, in a work published posthumously in 1821, her *Dix Années d'exil* (*Ten Years' Exile*). From December 1803 to April 1804, she made a journey through Germany, culminating in a visit to Weimar, already established as the shrine of J. W. von Goethe and Friedrich von Schiller. In Berlin, she met August Wilhelm von Schlegel, who was to become, after 1804, her frequent companion and counselor. Her guide in Germany, however, was a young Englishman, Henry Crabb Robinson, who was studying at Jena. The journey was interrupted in 1804 by news of the death of her father, whom she had always greatly admired. His death affected her deeply, but in 1805 she set out for Italy, accompanied by Schlegel and Simonde de Sismondi, the Genevan econo-mist who was her guide on the journey. Returning in June 1805, she spent the next seven years of her exile from Paris for the most part at Coppet.

While *Corinne* can be considered the result of her Italian journey, the fruits of her visit to Germany are contained in her most important work, *De l'Allemagne* (1810; *Germany*). This is a serious study of German manners, literature and art, philosophy and morals, and religion in which she made known to her contemporaries the Germany of the Sturm und Drang movement (1770–1780). Its only fault is the dis-torted picture it gives, ignoring, for example, the violently nationalistic aspect of German Romanticism. Napoleon took it for an anti-French work, and the French edition of 1810 (10,000 copies) was seized and destroyed. It was finally published in England in 1813.

Meanwhile Mme de Staël, persecuted by the police, fled from Napoleon's Europe. Having married, in 1811, a young Swiss officer, "John" Rocca, in May 1812 she went to Austria and, after visiting Russia, Finland, and Sweden, arrived, in June 1813, in England. She was received with enthusiasm, although reproached by such liberals as Lord Byron for being more anti-Napoleonic than liberal and by the Tories for being too liberal. Her guide in England was Sir James Mackintosh, the Scottish publicist. She collected documents for, but never wrote, a *De l'Angleterre*: (the material for it can be found in the *Considérations sur la Révolution française* [1818; *Considerations on the Principal Events of the French Revolution*], which represents a return to Necker's ideas and holds up the English political system as a model for France).

On the Bourbon Restoration in 1814, Mme de Staël returned to Paris but was deeply disillusioned: the fall of Napoleon had been followed by foreign occupation and had in no way reestablished liberty in France. During the Hundred Days, she escaped to Coppet and in September 1815 set out again for Italy. In 1816, she returned to spend the summer at Coppet, where she was joined by Byron, in flight from England after his unhappy matrimonial experience. A strong friendship developed between the two writers.

Madame de Staël's health was declining. After Byron's departure, she went to Paris for the winter. Though poorly received by the returned émigrés and suspected by the government, she held her salon throughout the winter and part of the spring, but after April 1817 she was an invalid. She died in Paris in July of that year.

ASSESSMENT

Germaine de Staël's purely literary importance is far exceeded by her importance in the history of ideas. Her novels and plays are now largely forgotten, but the value of her critical and historical work is undeniable. Though careless of detail, she had a clear vision of wider issues and of the achievements of civilization. Her involvement in, and understanding of, the events and tendencies of her time gave her an unusual position: it may be said that she helped the dawning 19th century to take stock of itself.

JANE AUSTEN

(b. Dec. 16, 1775, Steventon, Hampshire, Eng.—d. July 18, 1817, Winchester, Hampshire)

The English writer Jane Austen was the first writer to give the novel its distinctly modern character through her treatment of ordinary people in everyday life. Austen created the comedy of manners of middle-class life in the England of her time in her novels, *Sense and Sensibility* (1811), *Pride and Prejudice* (1813), *Mansfield Park* (1814), *Emma* (1815), and *Northanger Abbey* and *Persuasion* (published posthumously, 1817).

LIFE

Jane Austen was born in the Hampshire village of Steventon, where her father, the Reverend George Austen, was rector. She was the second daughter and seventh child in a family of eight: six boys and two girls. Her closest companion throughout her life was her elder sister, Cassandra, who also remained unmarried. Their father was a scholar who encouraged the love of learning in his children. His wife, Cassandra (née Leigh), was a woman of ready wit, famed for her impromptu verses and stories. The great family amusement was acting.

Jane Austen's lively and affectionate family circle provided a stimulating context for her writing. Moreover, her experience was carried far beyond Steventon rectory by an extensive network of relationships by blood and friendship. It was this world—of the minor landed gentry and the country clergy, in the village, the neighborhood, and the country town, with occasional visits to Bath and to London—that she was to use in the settings, characters, and subject matter of her novels.

Her earliest-known writings date from about 1787, and between then and 1793 she wrote a large body of material that has survived in three manuscript notebooks: *Volume the First*, *Volume the Second*, and *Volume the Third*. These contain plays, verses, short novels, and other prose that show Austen engaged in the parody of existing literary forms, notably sentimental fiction. Her passage to a more serious view of life from the exuberant high spirits and extravagances of her earliest writings is evident in *Lady Susan*, a short novel-in-letters written about 1793–94 (and not published until 1871). This portrait of a woman bent on the exercise of her own powerful mind and personality to the point of social self-destruction is, in effect, a study of frustration and of woman's fate in a society that has no use for a woman's stronger, more "masculine," talents.

In 1802, it seems likely that Jane agreed to marry Harris Bigg-Wither, the 21-year-old heir of a Hampshire family, but the next morning changed her mind. There are also a number of mutually contradictory stories connecting her with someone with whom she fell in love but who died very soon after. Since Austen's novels are so deeply concerned with love and marriage, there is some point in attempting to establish the facts of these relationships. Unfortunately, the evidence is unsatisfactory and incomplete. Cassandra was a jealous guardian of her sister's private life, and after Jane's death she censored the surviving letters, destroying many and cutting up others. But Jane Austen's own novels provide indisputable evidence that their author understood the experience of love and of love disappointed.

The earliest of her novels, *Sense and Sensibility*, was begun about 1795 as a novel-in-letters called "Elinor and Marianne," after its heroines. Between October 1796 and August 1797, Austen completed the first version of *Pride and Prejudice*, then called "First Impressions." In 1797, her father wrote to offer it to a London publisher for publication, but the offer was declined. *Northanger Abbey*, the last of the early novels, was written about 1798 or 1799, probably under the title "Susan." In 1803 the manuscript of "Susan" was sold to the publisher Richard Crosby for £10. He took it for immediate publication, but, although it was advertised, unaccountably it never appeared.

Up to this time, the tenor of life at Steventon rectory had been propitious for Jane Austen's growth as a novelist. This stable environment ended in 1801, however, when George Austen, then aged 70, retired to Bath with his wife and daughters. For eight years, Jane had to put up with a succession of temporary lodgings or visits to relatives, in Bath, London, Clifton, Warwickshire, and, finally, Southampton, where the three women lived from 1805 to 1809. In 1804, Jane began *The Watsons* but soon abandoned it. Also in 1804, her dearest friend, Mrs. Anne Lefroy, died suddenly, and in January 1805 her father died in Bath.

Eventually, in 1809, Jane's brother Edward was able to provide his mother and sisters with a large cottage in the village of Chawton, within his Hampshire estate, not far from Steventon. The prospect of settling at Chawton had already given Jane Austen a renewed sense of purpose, and she began to prepare *Sense and Sensibility* and *Pride and Prejudice* for publication. She was encouraged by her brother Henry, who acted as go-between with her publishers. She was probably also prompted by her need for money. Two years later, Thomas Egerton agreed to publish *Sense and Sensibility*, which came out, anonymously, in November 1811. Both of the leading reviews, the *Critical*

Review and the *Quarterly Review*, welcomed its blend of instruction and amusement. Meanwhile, in 1811 Austen had begun *Mansfield Park*, which was finished in 1813 and published in 1814. By then she was an established (though anonymous) author; Egerton had published *Pride and Prejudice* in January 1813, and later that year there were second editions of *Pride and Prejudice* and *Sense and Sensibility*. *Pride and Prejudice* seems to have been the fashionable novel of its season. Between January 1814 and March 1815, she wrote *Emma*, which appeared in December 1815. In 1816, there was a second edition of *Mansfield Park*, published, like *Emma*, by Lord Byron's publisher, John Murray. *Persuasion* (written August 1815–August 1816) was published posthumously, with *Northanger Abbey*, in December 1817.

The years after 1811 seem to have been the most rewarding of her life. She had the satisfaction of seeing her work in print and well reviewed and of knowing that the novels were widely read. They were so much enjoyed by the Prince Regent (later George IV) that he had a set in each of his residences; *Emma*, at a discreet royal command, was "respectfully dedicated" to him. The reviewers praised the novels for their morality and entertainment, admired the character drawing, and welcomed the homely realism as a refreshing change from the romantic melodrama then in vogue.

For the last 18 months of her life, Austen was busy writing. Early in 1816, at the onset of her fatal illness, she set down the burlesque *Plan of a Novel, According to Hints from Various Quarters* (first published in 1871). Until August 1816, she was occupied with *Persuasion*, and she looked again at the manuscript of "Susan" (*Northanger Abbey*).

In January 1817, she began *Sanditon*, a robust and self-mocking satire on health resorts and invalidism. This novel remained unfinished owing to Austen's declining health. She supposed that she was suffering from bile, but the symptoms make possible a modern clinical assessment that she was suffering from Addison's disease. Her condition fluctuated, but in April she made her will, and in May she was taken to Winchester to be under the care of an expert surgeon. She died on July 18, and six days later she was buried in Winchester Cathedral.

Her authorship was announced to the world at large by her brother Henry, who supervised the publication of *Northanger Abbey* and *Persuasion*. There was no recognition at the time that regency England had lost its keenest observer and sharpest analyst; no understanding that a miniaturist (as she maintained that she was and as she was then seen), a "merely domestic" novelist, could be seriously concerned with the nature of society and the quality of its culture; no grasp of Jane Austen as a historian of the emergence of regency society into the modern world. During her lifetime there had been a solitary response in any way adequate to the nature of her achievement: Sir Walter Scott's review of *Emma* in the *Quarterly Review* for March 1816, where he hailed this "nameless author" as a masterful exponent of "the modern novel" in the new realist tradition. After her death, there was for long only one significant essay, the review of *Northanger Abbey* and *Persuasion* in the *Quarterly* for January 1821 by the theologian Richard Whately. Together, Scott's and Whately's essays provided the foundation for serious criticism of Jane Austen: their insights were appropriated by critics throughout the 19th century.

Novels

Jane Austen's three early novels form a distinct group in which a strong element of literary satire accompanies the comic depiction of character and society.

FROM THE LATE 1700S TO THE LATE 1800S
ELISABETH VIGÉE-LEBRUN TO FLORENCE NIGHTINGALE

Sense and Sensibility tells the story of the impoverished Dashwood sisters. Marianne is the heroine of "sensibility"— i.e., of openness and enthusiasm. She becomes infatuated with the attractive John Willoughby, who seems to be a romantic lover but is in reality an unscrupulous fortune hunter. He deserts her for an heiress, leaving her to learn a dose of "sense" in a wholly unromantic marriage with a staid and settled bachelor, Colonel Brandon, who is 20 years her senior. By contrast, Marianne's older sister, Elinor, is the guiding light of "sense," or prudence and discretion, whose constancy toward her lover, Edward Ferrars, is rewarded by her marriage to him after some distressing vicissitudes.

Pride and Prejudice describes the clash between Elizabeth Bennet, the daughter of a country gentleman, and Fitzwilliam Darcy, a rich and aristocratic landowner. Although Austen shows them intrigued by each other, she reverses the convention of "first impressions." "Pride" of rank and fortune and "prejudice" against Elizabeth's inferiority of family hold Darcy aloof, while Elizabeth is equally fired both by the "pride" of self-respect and by "prejudice" against Darcy's snobbery. Ultimately, they come together in love and self-understanding. The intelligent and high-spirited Elizabeth was Jane Austen's own favorite among all her heroines and is one of the most engaging in English literature.

Northanger Abbey combines a satire on conventional novels of polite society with one on Gothic tales of terror. Catherine Morland, the unspoiled daughter of a country parson, is the innocent abroad who gains worldly wisdom: first in the fashionable society of Bath and then at Northanger Abbey itself, where she learns not to interpret the world through her reading of Gothic thrillers. Her mentor and guide is the self-assured and gently ironic Henry Tilney, her husband-to-be.

In the three novels of Jane Austen's maturity, the literary satire, though still present, is more subdued and is subordinated to the comedy of character and society.

In its tone and discussion of religion and religious duty, *Mansfield Park* is the most serious of Austen's novels. The heroine, Fanny Price, is a self-effacing and unregarded cousin cared for by the Bertram family in their country house. Fanny emerges as a true heroine whose moral strength eventually wins her complete acceptance in the Bertram family and marriage to Edmund Bertram himself, after that family's disastrous involvement with the meretricious and loose-living Crawfords.

Of all Austen's novels, *Emma* is the most consistently comic in tone. It centers on Emma Woodhouse, a wealthy, pretty, self-satisfied young woman who indulges herself with meddlesome and unsuccessful attempts at matchmaking among her friends and neighbors. After a series of humiliating errors, a chastened Emma finds her destiny in marriage to the mature and protective George Knightley, a neighboring squire who had been her mentor and friend.

Persuasion tells the story of a second chance, the reawakening of love between Anne Elliot and Captain Frederick Wentworth, whom seven years earlier she had been persuaded not to marry. Now Wentworth returns from the Napoleonic Wars with prize money and the social acceptability of naval rank; he is an eligible suitor acceptable to Anne's snobbish father and his circle. Anne discovers the continuing strength of her love for him.

ASSESSMENT

Although the birth of the English novel is to be seen in the first half of the 18th century in the work of Daniel Defoe, Samuel Richardson, and Henry Fielding, it is with Jane

Austen that the novel takes on its distinctively modern character in the realistic treatment of unremarkable people in the unremarkable situations of everyday life. In her six novels—*Sense and Sensibility*, *Pride and Prejudice*, *Mansfield Park*, *Emma*, *Northanger Abbey*, and *Persuasion*—Austen created the comedy of manners of middle-class life in the England of her time, revealing the possibilities of "domestic" literature. Her repeated fable of a young woman's voyage to self-discovery on the passage through love to marriage focuses upon easily recognizable aspects of life. It is this concentration upon character and personality and upon the tensions between her heroines and their society that relates her novels more closely to the modern world than to the traditions of the 18th century. This modernity, together with the wit, realism, and timelessness of her prose style; her shrewd, amused sympathy; and the satisfaction to be found in stories so skillfully told, in novels so beautifully constructed, that helps to explain her continuing appeal for readers of all kinds. Modern critics remain fascinated by the commanding structure and organization of the novels, by the triumphs of technique that enable the writer to lay bare the tragicomedy of existence in stories of which the events and settings are apparently so ordinary and so circumscribed.

SACAGAWEA

(b. *ca.* 1788, near the Continental Divide at the present-day Idaho-Montana border [U.S.]—d. Dec. 20, 1812?, Fort Manuel, on the Missouri River, Dakota Territory)

Acting as an interpreter for the Lewis and Clark Expedition (1804–06), the Shoshone Indian woman Sacagawea traveled thousands of wilderness miles, from the Mandan-Hidatsa villages in the Dakotas to the Pacific Northwest.

Separating fact from legend in Sacagawea's life is difficult; historians disagree on the dates of her birth and death and even on her name. In Hidatsa, Sacagawea (pronounced with a hard *g*) translates into "Bird Woman." Alternatively, Sacajawea means "Boat Launcher" in Shoshone. Others favor Sakakawea. The Lewis and Clark journals generally support the Hidatsa derivation.

A Lemhi Shoshone woman, Sacagawea was about 12 years old when a Hidatsa raiding party captured her near the Missouri River's headwaters about 1800. Enslaved and taken to their Knife River earth-lodge villages near present-day Bismarck, North Dakota, she was purchased by French Canadian fur trader Toussaint Charbonneau and became one of his plural wives about 1804. They resided in one of the Hidatsa villages, Metaharta.

When explorers Meriwether Lewis and William Clark arrived at the Mandan-Hidatsa villages and built Fort Mandan to spend the winter of 1804–05, they hired Charbonneau as an interpreter to accompany them to the Pacific Ocean. Because he did not speak Sacagawea's language and because the expedition party needed to communicate with the Shoshones to acquire horses to cross the mountains, the explorers agreed that the pregnant Sacagawea should also accompany them. On February 11, 1805, she gave birth to a son, Jean Baptiste.

Departing on April 7, the expedition ascended the Missouri. On May 14, Charbonneau nearly capsized the white pirogue (boat) in which Sacagawea was riding. Remaining calm, she retrieved important papers, instruments, books, medicine, and other indispensable valuables that otherwise would have been lost. During the next week, Lewis and Clark named a tributary of Montana's Mussellshell River "Sah-ca-gah-weah," or "Bird Woman's River," after her. She proved to be a significant asset in numerous ways: searching for edible plants, making moccasins and clothing, as well as allaying suspicions of approaching Native American tribes through her presence; a woman and child accompanying a party of men indicated peaceful intentions.

By mid-August, the expedition encountered a band of Shoshones led by Sacagawea's brother Cameahwait. The reunion of sister and brother had a positive effect on Lewis and Clark's negotiations for the horses and guide that enabled them to cross the Rocky Mountains. Upon arriving at the Pacific coast, she was able to voice her opinion about where the expedition should spend the winter and was granted her request to visit the ocean to see a beached whale. She and Clark were fond of each other and performed numerous acts of kindness for one another, but romance between them occurred only in latter-day fiction.

Sacagawea was not the guide for the expedition, as some have erroneously portrayed her; nonetheless, she recognized landmarks in southwestern Montana and informed Clark that Bozeman Pass was the best route between the Missouri and Yellowstone rivers on their return journey. On July 25, 1806, Clark named Pompey's Tower (now Pompey's Pillar) on the Yellowstone after her son, whom Clark fondly called his "little dancing boy, Pomp."

The Charbonneau family disengaged from the expedition party upon their return to the Mandan-Hidatsa villages; Charbonneau eventually received $409.16 and 320 acres (130 hectares) for his services. Clark wanted to do more for their family, so he offered to assist them, eventually securing Charbonneau a position as an interpreter. The family traveled to Saint Louis in 1809 to baptize their son and left him in the care of Clark, who had earlier offered to provide him with an education. Shortly after the birth of a daughter named Lisette, a woman identified only as Charbonneau's wife (but believed to be Sacagawea) died at the end of 1812 at Fort Manuel, near present-day Mobridge, South Dakota. Clark became the legal guardian of Lisette and Jean Baptiste and listed Sacagawea as deceased in a list he compiled in the 1820s. Some biographers and oral traditions contend that it was another of Charbonneau's wives who died in 1812 and that Sacagawea went to live among the Comanches, started another family, rejoined the Shoshones, and died on Wyoming's Wind River Reservation on April 9, 1884. These accounts can likely be attributed to other Shoshone women who shared similar experiences as Sacagawea.

Sacagawea's son, Jean Baptiste, traveled throughout Europe before returning to enter the fur trade. He scouted for explorers and helped guide the Mormon Battalion to California before becoming an alcalde, a hotel clerk, and a gold miner. Lured to the Montana goldfields following the Civil War, he died en route near Danner, Oregon, on May 16, 1866. Little is known of Lisette's whereabouts prior to her death on June 16, 1832; she was buried in the Old Catholic Cathedral Cemetery in Saint Louis. Charbonneau died on August 12, 1843.

Sacagawea has been memorialized with statues, monuments, stamps, and place names. In 2000, her likeness appeared on a gold-tinted dollar coin struck by the U.S. Mint. In 2001, U.S. President Bill Clinton granted her a posthumous decoration as an honorary sergeant in the regular army.

SOJOURNER TRUTH

(b. *ca.* 1797, Ulster county, N.Y., U.S. — d. Nov. 26, 1883, Battle Creek, Mich.)

The eloquent African American evangelist and reformer Sojourner Truth (her legal name was Isabella Van Wagener) applied her religious fervor to the abolitionist and women's rights movements.

FROM THE LATE 1700S TO THE LATE 1800S
ELISABETH VIGÉE-LEBRUN TO FLORENCE NIGHTINGALE

Isabella was the daughter of enslaved people and spent her childhood as an abused chattel of several enslavers. Her first language was Dutch. Between 1810 and 1827, she bore at least five children to a fellow enslaved person named Thomas. Just before New York state abolished slavery in 1827, she found refuge with Isaac Van Wagener, who set her free. With the help of Quaker friends, she waged a court battle in which she recovered her small son, who had been sold illegally into slavery in the South. About 1829, she went to New York City with her two youngest children, supporting herself through domestic employment.

Since childhood, Isabella had had visions and heard voices, which she attributed to God. In New York City, she became associated with Elijah Pierson, a zealous missionary. Working and preaching in the streets, she joined his Retrenchment Society and his household.

In 1843, she left New York City and took the name Sojourner Truth, which she used from then on. Obeying a supernatural call to "travel up and down the land," she sang, preached, and debated at camp meetings, in churches, and on village streets, exhorting her listeners to accept the biblical message of God's goodness and the brotherhood of man. In the same year, she was introduced to abolitionism at a utopian community in Northampton, Massachusetts, and thereafter spoke in behalf of the movement throughout the state. In 1850, she traveled throughout the Midwest, where her reputation for personal magnetism preceded her and drew heavy crowds. She supported herself by selling copies of her book, *The Narrative of Sojourner Truth*, which she had dictated to Olive Gilbert.

Encountering the women's rights movement in the early 1850s, and encouraged by other women leaders, notably Lucretia Mott, she continued to appear before suffrage gatherings for the rest of her life. Sometime in the 1850s,

Sojourner Truth settled in Battle Creek, Michigan. At the beginning of the American Civil War, she gathered supplies for black volunteer regiments and in 1864 went to Washington, D.C., where she helped integrate streetcars and was received at the White House by President Abraham Lincoln. The same year, she accepted an appointment with the National Freedmen's Relief Association counseling former slaves, particularly in matters of resettlement. As late as the 1870s, she encouraged the migration of freedmen to Kansas and Missouri. In 1875, she retired to her home in Battle Creek, where she remained until her death in 1883.

DOROTHEA DIX

(b. April 4, 1802, Hampden, District of Maine, Mass. [now in Maine], U.S.—d. July 17, 1887, Trenton, N.J.)

The American educator, social reformer, and humanitarian Dorothea Dix led the fight for the welfare of the mentally ill, and her efforts led to widespread reforms in the United States and abroad.

Dorothea Lynde Dix left her unhappy home at age 12 to live and study in Boston with her grandmother. By age 14, she was teaching in a school for young girls in Worcester, Massachusetts, employing a curriculum of her own devising that stressed the natural sciences and the responsibilities of ethical living. In 1821, she opened a school for girls in Boston, where until the mid-1830s, periods of intensive teaching were interrupted by periods of ill health for Dix. She eventually abandoned teaching and left Boston.

After nearly two years in England, Dix returned to Boston, still a semi-invalid, and found to her amazement that she had inherited a sum of money sufficient to support her comfortably for life. But her Calvinist beliefs enjoined

FROM THE LATE 1700S TO THE LATE 1800S
ELISABETH VIGÉE-LEBRUN TO FLORENCE NIGHTINGALE

her from inactivity. Thus in 1841, when a young clergyman asked her to begin a Sunday school class in the East Cambridge House of Correction in Massachusetts, she accepted the challenge. In the prison, she first observed the inhumane treatment of insane and mentally disturbed persons, who were incarcerated with criminals, irrespective of age or sex. They were left unclothed, in darkness, without heat or sanitary facilities; some were chained to the walls and flogged. Profoundly shocked, Dix traveled for nearly two years throughout the state, observing similar conditions in each institution she examined. In January 1843, she submitted a detailed report of her thoroughly documented findings to the Massachusetts legislature. Her dignity, compassion, and determination were effective in helping to pass a bill for the enlargement of the Worcester Insane Asylum. Dix moved on to Rhode Island and New York.

In the next 40 years, Dix inspired legislators in 15 U.S. states and in Canada to establish state hospitals for the mentally ill. Her unflagging efforts directly effected the building of 32 institutions in the United States. She carried on her work even while on a convalescent tour of Europe in 1854–56, notably in Italy, where she prevailed upon Pope Pius IX to inspect personally the atrocious conditions she had discovered. Where new institutions were not required, she fostered the reorganization, enlargement, and restaffing—with well-trained, intelligent personnel— of already existing hospitals.

In 1845, Dix published *Remarks on Prisons and Prison Discipline in the United States* to advocate reforms in the treatment of ordinary prisoners. In 1861, she was appointed superintendent of army nurses for Civil War service. She was ill-suited to administration, however, and had great difficulty with the post. After the war, she returned to her work with hospitals. When she died, it was in a hospital that she had founded.

CHARLOTTE AND EMILY BRONTË

(Respectively, b. April 21, 1816, Thornton, Yorkshire, Eng.—
d. March 31, 1855, Haworth, Yorkshire; b. July 30, 1818, Thornton,
Yorkshire, Eng.—d. Dec. 19, 1848, Haworth, Yorkshire)

Charlotte Brontë and Emily Brontë, were English writers whose works—notably *Jane Eyre* (1847; by Charlotte) and *Wuthering Heights* (1847; by Emily)—are considered classics of English literature. Their youngest sister, Anne, was also a writer, the author of *Agnes Grey* (1847) and *The Tenant of Wildfell Hall* (1848), but her works are little known.

The Brontë sisters' father was Patrick Brontë (1777–1861), an Anglican clergyman. Irish-born, he had changed his name from the more commonplace Brunty. After serving in several parishes, he moved with his wife, Maria Branwell Brontë, and their six small children to Haworth amid the Yorkshire moors in 1820, having been awarded a rectorship there. Soon after, Mrs. Brontë and the two eldest children (Maria and Elizabeth) died, leaving the father to care for the remaining three girls—Charlotte, Emily, and Anne—and a boy, Patrick Branwell. Their upbringing was aided by an aunt, Elizabeth Branwell, who left her native Cornwall and took up residence with the family at Haworth.

In 1824, Charlotte and Emily, together with their elder sisters before their deaths, attended Clergy Daughters' School at Cowan Bridge, near Kirkby Lonsdale, Lancashire. The fees were low, the food unattractive, and the discipline harsh. Charlotte condemned the school (perhaps exaggeratedly) long years afterward in *Jane Eyre*, under the thin disguise of Lowood; and the principal, the Reverend William Carus Wilson, has been accepted as the counterpart of Mr. Brocklehurst in the novel.

Charlotte and Emily returned home in June 1825, and for more than five years the Brontë children learned

From the Late 1700s to the Late 1800s
Elisabeth Vigée-Lebrun to Florence Nightingale

and played there, writing and telling romantic tales for
one another and inventing imaginative games played out
at home or on the desolate moors.

It is at this point that their paths diverged somewhat.

Charlotte Brontë's Life

In 1831, Charlotte was sent to Miss Wooler's school at Roe
Head, near Huddersfield, where she stayed a year and
made some lasting friendships; her correspondence with
one of her friends, Ellen Nussey, continued until her
death, and has provided much of the current knowledge
of her life. In 1832, she came home to teach her sisters but
in 1835 returned to Roe Head as a teacher. She wished to
improve her family's position, and this was the only outlet
that was offered to her unsatisfied energies. Branwell,
moreover, was to start on his career as an artist, and it
became necessary to supplement the family resources.
The work, with its inevitable restrictions, was unconge-
nial to Charlotte. She fell into ill health and melancholia
and in the summer of 1838 terminated her engagement.

In 1839, Charlotte declined a proposal from the
Reverend Henry Nussey, her friend's brother, and some
months later one from another young clergyman. At the
same time Charlotte's ambition to make the practical
best of her talents and the need to pay Branwell's debts
urged her to spend some months as governess with the
Whites at Upperwood House, Rawdon. Branwell's talents
for writing and painting, his good classical scholarship,
and his social charm had engendered high hopes for him;
but he was fundamentally unstable, weak willed, and
intemperate. He went from job to job and took refuge in
alcohol and opium.

Meanwhile his sisters had planned to open a school
together, which their aunt had agreed to finance, and in

February 1842 Charlotte and Emily went to Brussels as pupils to improve their qualifications in French and acquire some German. The talent displayed by both brought them to the notice of Constantin Héger, a fine teacher and a man of unusual perception. After a brief trip home upon the death of her aunt, Charlotte returned to Brussels as a pupil-teacher. She stayed there during 1843 but was lonely and depressed. Her friends had left Brussels, and Madame Héger appears to have become jealous of her. The nature of Charlotte's attachment to Héger and the degree to which she understood herself have been much discussed. His was the most interesting mind she had yet met, and he had perceived and evoked her latent talents. His strong and eccentric personality appealed both to her sense of humor and to her affections. She offered him an innocent but ardent devotion, but he tried to repress her emotions. The letters she wrote to him after her return may well be called love letters. When, however, he suggested that they were open to misapprehension, she stopped writing and applied herself, in silence, to disciplining her feelings. However they are interpreted, Charlotte's experiences at Brussels were crucial for her development. She received a strict literary training, became aware of the resources of her own nature, and gathered material that served her, in various shapes, for all her novels.

In 1844, Charlotte attempted to start a school that she had long envisaged in the parsonage itself, as her father's failing sight precluded his being left alone. Prospectuses were issued, but no pupils were attracted to distant Haworth.

In the autumn of 1845, Charlotte came across some poems by Emily, and this led to the publication of a joint volume of *Poems by Currer, Ellis and Acton Bell* (1846), or Charlotte, Emily, and Anne; the pseudonyms were assumed to preserve secrecy and avoid the special

FROM THE LATE 1700S TO THE LATE 1800S
ELISABETH VIGÉE-LEBRUN TO FLORENCE NIGHTINGALE

Proving that (left to right) Anne, Emily, and Charlotte Brontë were not the only talented ones in the family, Branwell, their brother, painted the women's portrait in 1834.

treatment that they believed reviewers accorded to women. The book was issued at their own expense. It received few reviews and only two copies were sold. Nevertheless, a way had opened to them, and they were already trying to place the three novels they had written. Charlotte failed to place *The Professor: A Tale* but had, however, nearly finished *Jane Eyre: An Autobiography*, begun in August 1846 in Manchester, where she was staying with her father, who had gone there for an eye operation. When Smith, Elder and Company, declining *The Professor*, declared themselves willing to consider a three-volume novel with more action and excitement in it, she completed and submitted it at once. *Jane Eyre* was accepted, published less than eight weeks later (on October 16, 1847), and had an immediate success, far greater than that of the books that her sisters published the same year.

The months that followed were tragic ones. Branwell died in September 1848, Emily in December, and Anne in May 1849. Charlotte completed *Shirley: A Tale* in the empty parsonage, and it appeared in October. In the following years, Charlotte went three times to London as the guest of her publisher; there she met the novelist William Makepeace Thackeray and sat for her portrait by George Richmond. She stayed in 1851 with the writer Harriet Martineau and also visited her future biographer, Mrs. Elizabeth Gaskell, in Manchester and entertained her at Haworth. *Villette* came out in January 1853. Meanwhile, in 1851, she had declined a third offer of marriage, this time from James Taylor, a member of Smith, Elder and Company. Her father's curate, Arthur Bell Nicholls (1817–1906), an Irishman, was her fourth suitor. It took some months to win her father's consent, but they were married on June 29, 1854, in Haworth church. They spent their honeymoon in Ireland and then returned to Haworth, where her husband had pledged himself to continue as curate to her father. He did not share his wife's intellectual life, but she was happy to be loved for herself and to take up her duties as his wife. She began another book, *Emma*, of which some pages remain. Her pregnancy, however, was accompanied by exhausting sickness, and she died in 1855.

Charlotte's Works

Charlotte's first novel, *The Professor* (published posthumously, 1857), shows her sober reaction from the indulgences of her girlhood. Told in the first person by an English tutor in Brussels, it is based on Charlotte's experiences there, with a reversal of sexes and roles.

Though there is plenty of satire and dry, direct phrasing in *Jane Eyre*, its success was the fiery conviction with which it presented a thinking, feeling woman, craving for love but able to renounce it at the call of impassioned self-respect and moral conviction. The book's narrator and main character, Jane Eyre, is an orphan and is governess to the ward of Mr. Rochester, the Byronic and enigmatic employer with whom she falls in love. Her love is reciprocated, but on the wedding morning it comes out that Rochester is already married and keeps his mad and depraved wife in the attics of his mansion. Jane leaves him, suffers hardship, and finds work as a village schoolmistress. When Jane learns, however, that Rochester has been maimed and blinded while trying vainly to rescue his wife from the burning house that she herself had set afire, Jane seeks him out and marries him.

There are melodramatic naïvetés in the story, and Charlotte's elevated rhetorical passages do not much appeal to modern taste, but she maintains her hold on the reader. The novel is subtitled *An Autobiography* and is written in the first person; but, except in Jane Eyre's impressions of Lowood, the autobiography is not Charlotte's. Personal experience is fused with suggestions from widely different sources, and the Cinderella theme may well come from Samuel Richardson's *Pamela*. The action is carefully motivated, and apparently episodic sections, like the return to Gateshead Hall, are necessary to the full expression of Jane's character and the working out of the threefold moral theme of love, independence, and forgiveness.

In her novel *Shirley*, Charlotte avoided melodrama and coincidences and widened her scope. Setting aside Maria Edgworth and Sir Walter Scott as national novelists, *Shirley* is the first regional novel in English, full of shrewdly depicted local material—Yorkshire characters, church and chapel, the cloth workers and machine breakers of her father's early manhood, and a sturdy but rather embittered feminism.

In *Villette*, she recurred to the Brussels setting and the first-person narrative, disused in *Shirley*; the characters and incidents are largely variants of the people and life at the Pension Héger. Against this background she set the ardent heart, deprived of its object, contrasted with the woman happily fulfilled in love.

The influence of Charlotte's novels was much more immediate than that of *Wuthering Heights*. Her combination of romance and satiric realism had been the mode of nearly all the women novelists for a century. Her fruitful innovations were the presentation of a tale through the sensibility of a child or young woman, her lyricism, and the picture of love from a woman's standpoint.

EMILY BRONTË'S LIFE

In 1835, when Charlotte secured a teaching position at Miss Wooler's school at Roe Head, Emily accompanied her as a pupil but suffered from homesickness and remained only three months. In 1838, Emily spent six exhausting months as a teacher in Miss Patchett's school at Law Hill, near Halifax, and then resigned.

To keep the family together at home, Charlotte planned to keep a school for girls at Haworth. In February 1842, she and Emily went to Brussels to learn foreign languages and school management at the Pension Héger.

From the Late 1700s to the Late 1800s
Elisabeth Vigée-Lebrun to Florence Nightingale

Although Emily pined for home and for the wild moorlands, it seems that in Brussels she was better appreciated than Charlotte. In October, however, when her aunt died, Emily returned permanently to Haworth.

As recounted above, Charlotte's discovery that all three sisters—Charlotte, Emily, and Anne—had written verse led them to publish jointly a pseudonymous volume of verse, *Poems by Currer, Ellis and Acton Bell*; it contained 21 of Emily's poems, and a consensus of later criticism has accepted the fact that Emily's verse alone reveals true poetic genius.

By midsummer of 1847, Emily's *Wuthering Heights* and Anne's *Agnes Grey* had been accepted for joint publication by J. Cautley Newby of London, but publication was delayed until the appearance of their sister Charlotte's *Jane Eyre*, which was immediately and hugely successful. *Wuthering Heights*, when published in December 1847, did not fare well; critics were hostile, calling it too savage, too animal-like, and clumsy in construction. Only later did it come to be considered one of the finest novels in the English language.

Soon after the publication of her novel, Emily's health began to fail rapidly. She had been ill for some time, but now her breathing became difficult, and she suffered great pain. She died of tuberculosis in December 1848.

WUTHERING HEIGHTS

Emily Brontë's work on *Wuthering Heights* cannot be dated; she may well have spent a long time on this intense, solidly imagined novel. It is distinguished from other novels of the period by its dramatic and poetic presentation, its abstention from all comment by the author, and its unusual structure. It recounts in the retrospective narrative of an onlooker, which in turn includes shorter narratives, the impact of the waif Heathcliff on the two families of Earnshaw and Linton in a remote Yorkshire district at the end of the 18th century. Embittered by abuse and by the marriage of Cathy Earnshaw—who shares his stormy nature and whom he loves—to the gentle and prosperous Edgar Linton, Heathcliff plans a revenge on both families, extending into the second generation. Cathy's death in childbirth fails to set him free from his love-hate relationship with her, and the obsessive haunting persists until his death; the marriage of the surviving heirs of Earnshaw and Linton restores peace.

Sharing the family's dry humor and Charlotte's violent imagination, Emily diverges from her in making no use of the events of her own life and showing no preoccupation with her unmarried state or a governess's position. Working, like her, within a confined scene and with a small group of characters, she constructs an action, based on profound and primitive energies of love and hate, which proceeds logically and economically, making no use of such coincidences as Charlotte relies on, requiring no rich romantic similes or rhetorical patterns, and confining the superb dialogue to what is immediately relevant to the subject. The book's somber power and the elements of brutality in its characters puzzled and affronted some 19th-century opinion.

VICTORIA

(b. May 24, 1819, Kensington Palace, London, Eng.—d. Jan. 22, 1901, Osborne, near Cowes, Isle of Wight)

Victoria was queen of the United Kingdom of Great Britain and Ireland (1837–1901) and empress of India (1876–1901). She was the last monarch of the House of Hanover and gave her name to an era, the Victorian Age. During her reign, the English monarchy took on its modern ceremonial character. She and her husband, Prince Consort Albert of Saxe-Coburg-Gotha, had nine children, through whose marriages were descended many of the royal families of Europe. By the end of her reign, the longest in English history at that time, she had restored both dignity and popularity to a tarnished crown: an achievement of character, as well as of longevity. She will forever be noted for her high sense of duty, her transparent honesty, and the simplicity of her royal character.

Victoria first learned of her future role as a young princess during a history lesson when she was 10 years old. Almost four decades later, Victoria's governess recalled that the future queen reacted to the discovery by declaring, "I will be good." This combination of earnestness and egotism marked Victoria as a child of the age that bears her name. The queen, however, rejected important Victorian values and developments. Although she hated pregnancy and childbirth, detested babies, and was uncomfortable in the presence of children, Victoria reigned in a society that idealized both motherhood and the family. She had no interest in social issues, yet the 19th century in Britain was an age of reform. She resisted technological change even while mechanical and technological innovations reshaped the face of European civilization. Most significantly, Victoria was a queen determined to retain political power; yet unwillingly and unwittingly she presided over the transformation of the sovereign's political role into a ceremonial one and thus preserved the English monarchy.

Lineage and Early Life

On the death in 1817 of Princess Charlotte, daughter of the prince regent (later George IV), there was no surviving legitimate offspring of George III's 15 children. In 1818, therefore, three of his sons, the dukes of Clarence, Kent, and Cambridge, married to provide for the succession. The winner in the race to father the next ruler of Britain was Edward, duke of Kent, fourth son of King George III. His only child was christened Alexandrina Victoria. After his death and George IV's accession in 1820, Victoria became third in the line to the throne after the duke of York (died 1827) and the duke of Clarence (subsequently William IV), whose own children died in infancy.

Victoria, by her own account, "was brought up very simply," principally at Kensington Palace. An important father figure to the orphaned princess was her uncle Leopold, her mother's brother, who lived at Claremont, near Esher, Surrey, until he became king of the Belgians in 1831. Victoria's childhood was made increasingly unhappy by the machinations of Sir John Conroy, an adviser to her German-born mother, the duchess of Kent. Persuaded by Conroy that the royal dukes posed a threat to her daughter, the duchess systematically isolated Victoria from her contemporaries and her father's family. Despite this treatment, the strong-willed girl carried on, and when she ascended the throne in 1837, she did so alone.

ACCESSION TO THE THRONE

On June 20, 1837, Victoria learned of the death of William IV, third son of George III, and she became queen. As such, she, who had never before had a room to herself, exiled her mother to a distant set of apartments when they moved into Buckingham Palace. Conroy was pensioned off. Even her beloved uncle Leopold was politely warned off discussions of English politics. "Alone" at last, she enjoyed her newfound freedom.

She later came to feel that it was "the least sensible and satisfactory time in her whole life"; but at the time it was exciting and enjoyable, the more so because of her romantic friendship with Lord Melbourne, the prime minister.

Melbourne was a crucial influence on Victoria, in many ways an unfortunate one. The urbane and sophisticated prime minister fostered the new queen's self-confidence and enthusiasm for her role; he also encouraged her to ignore or minimize social problems and to attribute all discontent and unrest to the activities of a small group of agitators. Moreover, because of Melbourne, Victoria became an ardent Whig.

Her constitutionally dangerous political partisanship contributed to the first two crises of her reign, both of which broke in 1839. The Hastings affair began when Lady Flora Hastings, a maid of honor who was allied and connected to the Tories, was forced by Victoria to undergo a medical examination for suspected pregnancy. The gossip, when it was discovered that the queen had been mistaken, became the more damaging when later in the year Lady Flora died of a disease that had not been diagnosed by the examining physician. The enthusiasm of the populace over the coronation (June 28, 1838) swiftly dissipated.

Between the two phases of the Hastings case, "the bedchamber crisis" intervened. When Melbourne resigned in May 1839, Sir Robert Peel, the Conservative leader and Melbourne's apparent successor, stipulated that the Whig ladies of the bedchamber (household "ladies in waiting" to the queen) should be removed. The queen imperiously refused, not without Melbourne's encouragement, and Peel therefore declined to take office, which Melbourne rather weakly resumed. "I was very young then," wrote the queen long afterward, "and perhaps I should act differently if it was all to be done again."

MARRIAGE TO ALBERT

Attracted by Albert's good looks and encouraged by her

uncle Leopold, Victoria proposed to her cousin on October 15, 1839, just five days after he had arrived at Windsor on a visit to the English court. She described her impressions of him in the journal she kept: "Albert really is quite charming, and so extremely handsome . . . a beautiful figure, broad in the shoulders and a fine waist; my heart is quite *going.*" They were married on February 10, 1840, the queen dressed entirely in articles of British manufacture.

Children quickly followed. Victoria, the princess royal, was born in 1840; in 1858 she married the crown prince of Prussia and later became the mother of the emperor William II. The Prince of Wales (later Edward VII) was born in 1841. Then followed Princess Alice, afterward grand duchess of Hesse, 1843; Prince Alfred, afterward duke of Edinburgh and duke of Saxe-Coburg-Gotha, 1844; Princess Helena (Princess Christian of Schleswig-Holstein), 1846; Princess Louise (duchess of Argyll), 1848; Prince Arthur (duke of Connaught), 1850; Prince Leopold (duke of Albany), 1853; and Princess Beatrice (Princess Henry of Battenberg), 1857. The queen's first grandchild was born in 1859, and her first great-grandchild in 1879. There were 37 great-grandchildren alive at her death.

Victoria never lost her early passion for Albert: "Without him everything loses its interest." Despite conflicts produced by the queen's uncontrollable temper and recurrent fits of depression, which usually occurred during and after pregnancy, the couple had a happy marriage. Victoria, however, was never reconciled to the childbearing that accompanied her marital bliss—the "shadow-side of marriage," as she called it.

At the beginning of their marriage, the queen was insistent that her husband should have no share in the government of the country. Within six months, on Melbourne's repeated suggestion, the prince was allowed to start seeing the dispatches, then to be present when the queen saw her ministers. The concession became a routine, and during her first pregnancy the prince received a "key to the secret boxes." As one unwanted pregnancy followed another and as Victoria became increasingly dependent on her husband, Albert assumed an ever-larger political role. Victoria, who was once so enthusiastic about her role, came to conclude that "we women are not *made* for governing."

THE ALBERTINE MONARCHY

The prince came into his own to negotiate with Peel a compromise on the bedchamber question after the Melbourne government had been defeated in the general election of 1841. The following year Albert became effectively the queen's private secretary—according to himself, "her permanent minister."

A visible sign of the prince's power and influence was the building of the royal residences of Osborne, on the Isle of Wight, and Balmoral Castle in Scotland between 1845 and 1855. Victoria described Osborne as "our island home" and retreated there frequently; it was, however, at Balmoral that she was happiest. She liked the simpler life of the Highlands, and she took delight in the plain speech of John Brown, the Highland servant who stalked with Albert and became her personal attendant.

The royal couple's withdrawal to Scotland and the Isle of Wight bore witness to a new sort of British monarchy. In their quest for privacy and intimacy, Albert and Victoria adopted a way of life that mirrored that of their middle-class subjects, admittedly on a grander scale. Although Albert was interested in intellectual and scientific matters, Victoria's tastes were closer to those of most of her people. She enjoyed the novels of Charles Dickens and patronized the circus and waxwork exhibitions. Both Victoria and

Albert, however, differed from many in the middle class in their shared preference for nudes in painting and sculpture. Victoria's tastes show she was not the prude that many claimed her to be.

Victoria's delight in mingling with the Scottish poor at Balmoral did little to raise the level of her social awareness. Although in 1846 she and Albert supported the repeal of the Corn Laws (protectionist legislation that kept the price of British grain artificially high) in order to relieve distress in famine-devastated Ireland, they remained much more interested in and involved with the building of Osborne and foreign policy than in the tragedy of Ireland. Victoria, moreover, gave her full support to the government's policy of repression of the Chartists (advocates of far-reaching political and social reform) and believed the workers in her realm to be contented and loyal.

For both the queen and the prince consort, the highlight of their reign came in 1851, with the opening of the Great Exhibition. Albert poured himself into the task of organizing the international trade show that became a symbol of the Victorian Age. Housed in the architectural marvel of the Crystal Palace, a splendid, greenhouse-inspired glass building erected in Hyde Park, the Great Exhibition displayed Britain's wealth and technological achievements to a wondering world.

FOREIGN AFFAIRS

By tradition, the sovereign had a special part to play in foreign affairs and could conduct them alone with a secretary of state. Victoria and Albert had relatives throughout Europe and were to have more. Moreover, they visited and were visited by other monarchs. Albert was determined that this personal intelligence should not be disregarded and that the queen should never become a mere figurehead who represented the will of the foreign minister. The result was a clash with Lord Palmerston, the foreign secretary, who could look back on a career of high office beginning before the royal couple was born.

Even after Victoria insisted to Palmerston in 1850, "having once given her sanction to a measure, that it be not arbitrarily altered or modified by the minister," the foreign secretary continued to follow policies disapproved of by both Albert and Victoria, such as his encouragement of nationalist movements that threatened to dismember the Austrian Empire. Finally, after Palmerston expressed his approval of the coup d'état of Louis Napoleon (later Napoleon III) in 1851 without consulting the queen, the prime minister, Lord John Russell, dismissed him. Within a few months, the immensely popular Palmerston was back in office as home secretary. He would serve twice as prime minister.

On the eve of the Crimean War (1854–56), the royal pair encountered a wave of unpopularity, but there was a marked revival of royalist sentiment as the war wore on. The queen personally superintended the committees of ladies who organized relief for the wounded and eagerly seconded the efforts of Florence Nightingale: she visited crippled soldiers in the hospitals and instituted the Victoria Cross for gallantry.

With the death of Prince Albert on December 14, 1861, the Albertine monarchy came to an end. Albert's influence on the queen was lasting. He had changed her personal habits and her political sympathies. From him, she had received training in orderly ways of business, in hard work, in the expectation of royal intervention in ministry making at home, and in the establishment of a private (because royal) intelligence service abroad. The English monarchy too had changed.

DISRAELI'S INFLUENCE

After Albert's death, Victoria descended into deep depression. Even after she conquered her depression, she remained in mourning and in partial retirement. She balked at performing the ceremonial functions expected of the monarch and withdrew to Balmoral and Osborne four months out of every year. After an initial period of respect and sympathy for the queen's grief, the public grew increasingly impatient with its absent sovereign.

Although Victoria resisted carrying out her ceremonial duties, she remained determined to retain an effective political role and to behave as Albert would have ordained. It was despite, yet because of, Albert that Victoria succumbed to Benjamin Disraeli. Albert had not liked him, but he was able to enter into the queen's grief, flatter her, restore her self-confidence, and make the lonely crown an easier burden. Behind all his calculated attacks on her affections there was a bond of mutual loneliness, a note of mystery and romanticism, and, besides, the return to good gossip. Disraeli, moreover, told the queen in 1868 that it would be "his delight and duty, to render the transaction of affairs as easy to your Majesty, as possible." Since the queen was only too ready to consider herself overworked, this approach was especially successful. On the other hand, the queen's former prime minister, William Gladstone, would never acknowledge that she was, as she put it, "dead beat," perhaps because he never was himself; Disraeli, however, tired easily. The contrast between Disraeli's lively, often malicious, gossipy letters and Gladstone's 40 sides of foolscap is obvious. And there was no Albert to give her a neat précis. The queen had no patience with Gladstone's moralistic (and, she believed, hypocritical) approach to politics and foreign affairs. His persistent and often tactless attempts to persuade her to resume her ceremonial duties especially enraged her.

Over the problem of Ireland their paths separated ever more widely. The queen (like the majority of her subjects) had little understanding of, or sympathy for, Irish grievances. In all, she made but four visits to Ireland. The news of Gladstone's defeat in 1874 delighted the queen.

One of the bonds shared by Victoria and Disraeli was a romantic attachment to the East and the idea of empire. The queen was entranced by his imperialism and by his assertive foreign policy. She applauded his brilliant maneuvering, which led to the British purchase of slightly less than half of the shares in the Suez Canal in 1875 (a move that prevented the canal from falling entirely under French control), especially since he presented the canal as a personal gift to her: "It is just settled; you have it, Ma'am." The addition of "Empress of India" in 1876 to the royal title thrilled the queen even more. Victoria and Disraeli also agreed on their answer to the vexing "Eastern question"—what was to be done with the declining Turkish empire? Both held that Britain's best interests lay in supporting Turkey, the "Sick Man" of Europe. The fact that Gladstone took the opposing view, of course, strengthened their pro-Turkish sympathies. With the outbreak of a Russo-Turkish war in 1877, however, Disraeli had to restrain his bellicose sovereign, who demanded that Britain enter the war against Russia. At the Congress of Berlin in 1878, Disraeli emerged triumphant: Russian influence in the Balkans was reduced, and Britain gained control of the strategically located island of Cyprus. The queen was ecstatic.

Victoria's delight in Disraeli's premiership made further conflict with Gladstone inevitable. When the Conservative Party was defeated in 1880, she made no secret of her hostility toward Gladstone. She hoped he would retire, and she remained in correspondence with

Lord Beaconsfield (as Disraeli had become). Despite her feelings about leading what she scornfully called a "Democratic Monarchy," Victoria did act as an important mediating influence between the two houses to bring about the compromise that resulted in the third parliamentary Reform Act in 1884.

Victoria never acclimatized herself to the effects of the new electorate on party organization. No longer was the monarchy normally necessary as cabinet maker. Yet the queen was reluctant to accept her more limited role. Thus, in 1886 she sought to avoid a third Gladstone ministry by attempting to form an anti-Radical coalition. Her attempt failed.

LAST YEARS

In the Salisbury administration (1895–1902), with which her long reign ended, Victoria was eventually to find not only the sort of ministry with which she felt comfortable but one which lent a last ray of color to her closing years by its alliance, through Joseph Chamberlain, with the mounting imperialism that she had so greatly enjoyed in Disraeli's day when he had made her empress of India.

The South African War (1899–1902) dominated her final years. The sufferings of her soldiers in South Africa aroused the queen to a level of activity and public visibility that she had avoided for decades. With a demanding schedule of troop inspections, medal ceremonies, and visits to military hospitals, Victoria finally became the exemplar of a modern monarch.

She remained, nevertheless, either aloof from or in opposition to many of the important political, social, and intellectual currents of the later Victorian period. She never reconciled herself to the advance of democracy, and she thought the idea of female suffrage anathema. The sufferings of an individual worker could engage her sympathy; the working class, however, remained outside her field of vision. Many of the movements of the day passed the aged queen by, many irritated her, but the stupendous hard work that Albert had taught her went on—the meticulous examination of the boxes, the regular signature of the papers. To the very end, Victoria remained a passionate and strong-willed woman.

Those nearest to her came completely under her spell; all from the Prince of Wales down stood in considerable awe. Those who suffered her displeasure never forgot it, nor did she. Yielding to nobody else's comfort and keeping every anniversary, she lived surrounded by mementos, photographs, miniatures, busts, and souvenirs in chilly rooms at the end of drafty corridors, down which one tiptoed past Indian attendants to the presence. Nobody knocked; a gentle scratching on the door was all that she permitted. Every night at Windsor, Albert's clothes were laid out on the bed, every morning fresh water was put in the basin in his room. She slept with a photograph—over her head—taken of his head and shoulders as he lay dead. When she died, after a short and painless illness, she was buried beside Prince Albert in the mausoleum at Frogmore near Windsor.

SUSAN B. ANTHONY AND ELIZABETH CADY STANTON

(Respectively, b. Feb. 15, 1820, Adams, Mass., U.S.—d. March 13, 1906, Rochester, N.Y.; b. Nov. 12, 1815, Johnstown, N.Y., U.S.—d. Oct. 26, 1902, New York, N.Y.)

Susan B. Anthony and Elizabeth Cady Stanton led the women's rights movement and were crusaders for women's suffrage in the United States. Their work helped pave the way for the 19th Amendment (1920) to the

Constitution, giving women the right to vote.

SUSAN B. ANTHONY

Susan Brownell Anthony was reared in the Quaker tradition in a home pervaded by a tone of independence and moral zeal. She was a precocious child and learned to read and write at age three. After the family moved from Massachusetts to Battensville, New York, in 1826, she attended a district school, then a school set up by her father, and finally a boarding school near Philadelphia. In 1839, she took a position in a Quaker seminary in New Rochelle, New York. After teaching at a female academy in upstate New York (1846–49), she settled in her family home, now near Rochester, New York. There she met many leading abolitionists, including Frederick Douglass, Parker Pillsbury, Wendell Phillips, William Henry Channing, and William Lloyd Garrison. Soon the temperance movement enlisted her sympathy; after meeting Amelia Bloomer and, through her, Elizabeth Cady Stanton, so did that of women's suffrage.

The rebuff of Anthony's attempt to speak at a temperance meeting in Albany in 1852 prompted her to organize the Woman's New York State Temperance Society, of which Stanton became president. The episode also pushed Anthony farther in the direction of women's rights advocacy. In a short time she became known as one of the cause's most zealous, serious advocates, a dogged and tireless worker whose personality contrasted sharply with that of her friend and coworker Stanton. She was also a prime target of public and newspaper abuse.

While campaigning for a liberalization of New York's laws regarding married women's property rights, an end attained in 1860, Anthony served from 1856 as chief New York agent of Garrison's American Anti-Slavery Society.

During the early phase of the Civil War she helped organize the Women's National Loyal League, which urged the case for emancipation. After the war she campaigned unsuccessfully to have the language of the 14th Amendment altered to allow for woman as well as African American suffrage, and in 1866 she became corresponding secretary of the newly formed American Equal Rights Association. Her exhausting speaking and organizing tour of Kansas in 1867 failed to win passage of a state enfranchisement law.

In 1868, Anthony became publisher, and Stanton editor, of a new periodical, *The Revolution*, originally financed by the eccentric George Francis Train. The same year, she represented the Working Women's Association of New York, which she had recently organized, at the National Labor Union convention. In January 1869, she organized a women's suffrage convention in Washington, D.C., and in May she and Stanton formed the National Woman Suffrage Association (NWSA). A portion of the organization deserted later in the year to join Lucy Stone's more conservative American Woman Suffrage Association, but the NWSA remained a large and powerful group and Anthony remained its principal leader and spokeswoman.

In 1870, she relinquished her position at *The Revolution* and embarked on a series of lecture tours to pay off the paper's accumulated debts. As a test of the legality of the suffrage provision of the 14th Amendment, she cast a vote in the 1872 presidential election in Rochester, New York. She was arrested, convicted (the judge's directed verdict of guilty had been written before the trial began), and fined, and although she refused to pay the fine the case was carried no further. She traveled constantly, often with Stanton, in support of efforts in various states to win the franchise for women: California in 1871, Michigan in 1874, Colorado in 1877, and elsewhere. In 1890, after lengthy discussions, the rival suffrage associations were merged into the National American Woman Suffrage Association, and at Stanton's resignation in 1892 Anthony became president. Her principal lieutenant in later years was Carrie Chapman Catt.

By the 1890s, Anthony had largely outlived the abuse and sarcasm that had attended her early efforts, and she emerged as a national heroine. Her visits to the World's Columbian Exposition in Chicago in 1893 and to the Lewis and Clark Exposition in Portland, Oregon, in 1905 were warmly received, as were her trips to London in 1899 and Berlin in 1904 as head of the U.S. delegation to the international Council of Women (which she helped found in 1888). In 1900, at the age of 80, she retired from the presidency of the National American Woman Suffrage Association, passing it on to Catt.

Principal among Anthony's written works are the first four volumes of the six-volume *History of Woman Suffrage*, written with Stanton and Matilda J. Gage. Various of her writings are collected in *The Elizabeth Cady Stanton-Susan B. Anthony Reader* (1992), edited by Ellen Carol DuBois, and *The Selected Papers of Elizabeth Cady Stanton and Susan B. Anthony* (1997), edited by Ann D. Gordon. With the issue of a new dollar coin in 1979, she became the first woman to be depicted on U.S. currency, although the honor was somewhat mitigated by popular rejection of the coin because its size was so similar to that of the 25-cent coin.

ELIZABETH CADY STANTON

Elizabeth Cady received a superior education at home, at the Johnstown Academy, and at Emma Willard's Troy Female Seminary, from which she graduated in 1832. While studying law in the office of her father, Daniel Cady, a U.S.

FROM THE LATE 1700S TO THE LATE 1800S
ELISABETH VIGÉE-LEBRUN TO FLORENCE NIGHTINGALE

congressman and later a New York Supreme Court judge, she learned of the discriminatory laws under which women lived and determined to win equal rights for her sex.

In 1840, she married Henry Brewster Stanton, a lawyer and abolitionist (she insisted that the word *obey* be dropped from the wedding ceremony). Later that year they attended the World's Anti-Slavery Convention in London, and she was outraged at the denial of official recognition to several women delegates, notably Lucretia C. Mott, because of their sex. She became a frequent speaker on the subject of women's rights and circulated petitions that helped secure passage by the New York legislature in 1848 of a bill granting married women's property rights.

In 1848, she and Mott issued a call for a women's rights convention to meet in Seneca Falls, New York (where Stanton lived), on July 19–20 and in Rochester, New York, on subsequent days. At the meeting, Stanton introduced her Declaration of Sentiments, modeled on the Declaration of Independence, that detailed the inferior status of women and that, in calling for extensive reforms, effectively launched the American women's rights movement. She also introduced a resolution calling for women's suffrage that was adopted after considerable debate.

From 1851, she worked closely with Susan B. Anthony. Together they remained active for 50 years after the first convention, planning campaigns, speaking before legislative bodies, and addressing gatherings in conventions, in lyceums, and in the streets. Stanton, the better orator and writer, was perfectly complemented by Anthony, the organizer and tactician. She wrote not only her own and many of Anthony's addresses but also countless letters and pamphlets, as well as articles and essays for numerous periodicals, including Amelia Bloomer's *Lily*, Paulina Wright Davis's *Una*, and Horace Greeley's *New York Tribune*. In 1854, Stanton received an unprecedented invitation to

SUSAN B. ANTHONY AND ELIZABETH CADY STANTON

Susan B. Anthony (left) and Elizabeth Cady Stanton (right) worked together for 50 years as leaders of the women's rights movement.

FROM THE LATE 1700S TO THE LATE 1800S
ELISABETH VIGÉE-LEBRUN TO FLORENCE NIGHTINGALE

address the New York legislature. Her speech resulted in new legislation in 1860 granting married women the rights to their wages and to equal guardianship of their children.

During her presidency in 1852–53 of the short-lived Woman's State Temperance Society, which she and Anthony had founded, she scandalized many of her most ardent supporters by suggesting that drunkenness made sufficient cause for divorce. Liberalized divorce laws continued to be one of her principal issues.

During the Civil War, Stanton again worked for abolitionism. In 1863, she and Anthony organized the Women's National Loyal League, which gathered more than 300,000 signatures on petitions calling for immediate emancipation. The movement to extend the franchise to African American men after the war, however, caused her bitterness and outrage, reemphasized the disenfranchisement of women, and led her and her colleagues to redouble their efforts for women's suffrage.

Stanton and Anthony made several exhausting speaking and organizing tours on behalf of women's suffrage. In 1868, Stanton became coeditor (with Parker Pillsbury) of the newly established weekly *The Revolution*, a newspaper devoted to women's rights. She continued to write fiery editorials until the paper's demise in 1870. She helped organize the National Woman Suffrage Association in 1869 and was named its president, a post she retained until 1890, when the organization merged with the rival American Woman Suffrage Association. She was then elected president of the new National American Woman Suffrage Association and held that position until 1892.

Stanton continued to write and lecture tirelessly. She was the principal author of the Declaration of Rights for Women presented at the Centennial Exposition in Philadelphia in 1876. In 1878, she drafted a federal suffrage amendment that was introduced in every Congress thereafter until women were granted the right to vote in 1920. With Susan B. Anthony and Matilda Joslyn Gage, she compiled the first three volumes of the six-volume *History of Woman Suffrage*. She also published *The Woman's Bible*, 2 vol. (1895–98), and an autobiography, *Eighty Years and More* (1898).

FLORENCE NIGHTINGALE

(b. May 12, 1820, Florence [Italy]—d. Aug. 13, 1910, London, Eng.)

Florence Nightingale is best known as the foundational philosopher of modern nursing. She was also a statistician and social reformer.

Florence was a precocious child intellectually. Her father took particular interest in her education, guiding her through history, philosophy, and literature. She excelled in mathematics and languages and was able to read and write French, German, Italian, Greek, and Latin at an early age. Never satisfied with the traditional female skills of home management, she preferred to read the great philosophers and to engage in serious political and social discourse with her father.

As part of a liberal Unitarian family, Florence found great comfort in her religious beliefs. At the age of 16, she experienced one of several "calls from God." She viewed her particular calling as reducing human suffering. Nursing seemed the suitable route to serve both God and humankind. However, despite having cared for sick relatives and tenants on the family estates, her attempts to seek nurse's training were thwarted by her family as an inappropriate activity for a woman of her stature.

Nursing in Peace and War

Despite family reservations, Nightingale was eventually able to enroll at the Institution of Protestant Deaconesses at Kaiserswerth in Germany for two weeks of training in July 1850 and again for three months in July 1851. There she learned basic nursing skills, the importance of patient observation, and the value of good hospital organization. In 1853, Nightingale sought to break free from her family environment. Through social connections, she became the superintendent of the Institution for Sick Gentlewomen (governesses) in Distressed Circumstances, in London, where she successfully displayed her skills as an administrator by improving nursing care, working conditions, and efficiency of the hospital. After one year, she began to realize that her services would be more valuable in an institution that would allow her to train nurses. She considered becoming the superintendent of nurses at King's College Hospital in London. However, politics, not nursing expertise, was to shape her next move.

In October 1853, the Turkish Ottoman Empire declared war on Russia, following a series of disputes over holy places in Jerusalem and Russian demands to exercise protection over the Orthodox subjects of the Ottoman sultan. The British and the French, allies of Turkey, sought to curb Russian expansion. The majority of the Crimean War was fought on the Crimean Peninsula in Russia. However, the British troop base and hospitals for the care of the sick and wounded soldiers were primarily established in Scutari (Üsküdar), across the Bosporus from Constantinople (Istanbul). The status of the care of the wounded was reported to the London *Times* by the first modern war correspondent, British journalist William Howard Russell. The newspaper reports stated that soldiers were treated by an incompetent and ineffective medical establishment

FLORENCE NIGHTINGALE

Florence Nightingale was not only a nurse but also a social reformer who shaped the history of health care.

and that the most basic supplies were not available for care. The British public raised an outcry over the treatment of the soldiers and demanded that the situation be drastically improved.

Sidney Herbert, secretary of state at war for the British government, wrote to Nightingale requesting that she lead a group of nurses to Scutari. At the same time, Nightingale wrote to her friend Liz Herbert, Sidney's wife, asking that she be allowed to lead a private expedition. Their letters crossed in the mail, but in the end their mutual requests were granted. Nightingale led an officially sanctioned party of 38 women, departing October 21, 1854, and arriving in Scutari at the Barrack Hospital on November 5.

Not welcomed by the medical officers, Nightingale found conditions filthy, supplies inadequate, staff uncooperative, and overcrowding severe. Few nurses had access to the cholera wards, and Nightingale, who wanted to gain the confidence of army surgeons by waiting for official military orders for assistance, kept her party from the wards. Five days after Nightingale's arrival in Scutari, injured soldiers from the Battle of Balaklava and the Battle of Inkerman arrived and overwhelmed the facility. Nightingale said it was the "Kingdom of Hell."

In order to care for the soldiers properly, it was necessary that adequate supplies be obtained. Nightingale bought equipment with funds provided by the London *Times* and enlisted soldiers' wives to assist with the laundry. The wards were cleaned and basic care was provided by the nurses. Most important, Nightingale established standards of care, requiring such basic necessities as bathing, clean clothing and dressings, and adequate food. Attention was given to psychological needs through assistance in writing letters to relatives and through providing educational and recreational activities. Nightingale herself wandered the wards at night, providing support to the patients; this earned her the title of "Lady with the Lamp." She gained the respect of the soldiers and medical establishment alike. Her accomplishments in providing care and reducing the mortality rate to about 2 percent brought her fame in England through the press and through the soldiers' letters.

In May 1855, Nightingale began the first of several excursions to the Crimea; however, shortly after arriving, she fell ill with "Crimean fever"—most likely brucellosis, which she probably contracted from drinking contaminated milk. Nightingale experienced a slow recovery, as no active treatment was available. The lingering effects of the disease were to last for 25 years, frequently confining her to bed because of severe, chronic pain.

On March 30, 1856, the Treaty of Paris ended the Crimean War. Nightingale remained in Scutari until the hospitals were ready to close, returning to her home in Derbyshire on August 7, 1856, as a reluctant heroine.

Homecoming and Legacy

Although primarily remembered for her accomplishments during the Crimean War, Nightingale's greatest achievements centered on attempts to create social reform in health care and nursing. On her return to England, Nightingale was suffering the effects of both brucellosis and exhaustion. In September 1856, she met with Queen Victoria and Prince Albert to discuss the need for reform of the British military establishment. Nightingale kept meticulous records regarding the running of the Barrack Hospital, causes of illness and death, the efficiency of the nursing and medical staffs, and difficulties in purveyance. A Royal Commission was established, which based its findings on the statistical data and analysis provided by

FROM THE LATE 1700S TO THE LATE 1800S
ELISABETH VIGÉE-LEBRUN TO FLORENCE NIGHTINGALE

Nightingale. The result was marked reform in the military medical and purveyance systems.

In 1855, as a token of gratitude and respect for Nightingale, the Nightingale Fund was established. Through private donations, £45,000 was raised by 1859 and put at Nightingale's disposal. She used a substantial part of these monies to institute the Nightingale School of Nursing at Saint Thomas' Hospital in London, which opened in 1860. The school formalized secular nursing education, making nursing a viable and respectable option for women who desired employment outside of the home. The model was taken worldwide by matrons (women supervisors of public health institutions). Nightingale's statistical models—such as the Coxcomb chart, which she developed to assess mortality—and her basic concepts regarding nursing remain applicable today. For these reasons she is considered the foundational philosopher of modern nursing.

Nightingale improved the health of households through her most famous publication, *Notes on Nursing: What It Is and What It Is Not*, which provided direction on how to manage the sick. This volume has been in continuous publication worldwide since 1859. Additional reforms were financed through the Nightingale Fund, and a school for the education of midwives was established at King's College Hospital in 1862. Believing that the most important location for the care of the sick was in the home, she established training for district nursing, which was aimed at improving the health of the poor and vulnerable. A second Royal Commission examined the health of India, resulting in major environmental reform, again based on Nightingale's statistical data.

Florence Nightingale was honored in her lifetime by receiving the title of Lady of Grace of the Order of Saint John of Jerusalem and by becoming the first woman to receive the Order of Merit. On her death in 1910, at

FLORENCE NIGHTINGALE

Nightingale's prior request, her family declined the offer of a state funeral and burial in Westminster Abbey. Instead, she was honored with a memorial service at Saint Paul's Cathedral, London. Her burial is in the family plot in Saint Margaret's Church, East Wellow, Hampshire.

GLOSSARY

accession: The act of coming to power.

anathema: Something that is intensely disliked.

chattel: Objects and people that are considered someone's personal property.

foolscap: A standard sheet of writing or printing paper in England.

governess: A woman employed, usually in a private household, to teach someone's children and to act as their nanny.

meretricious: Superficially significant, showy but shallow.

parody: Imitating a style in such a way as to mock it.

précis: A short summary of important points.

Romanticism: An artistic movement of the late 18th century characterized by an emphasis on the individual, the subjective, the irrational, the imaginative, the personal, the spontaneous, the emotional, the visionary, and the transcendental.

salon: A meeting of notable people, usually artists, writers, and statesmen, held in someone's home.

satire: Something that makes fun of and shows the weaknesses of human nature.

suffrage: The right to vote.

utopian: An ideal but impractical situation, thought, or location.

vicissitude: A sudden or unexpected change in one's life; the ability of life to change quickly and without warning.

FOR MORE INFORMATION

BOOKS

Archer, Mandy. *Queen Victoria: Monarch, Champion of the Arts, Icon*. London, UK: Puffin, 2019.

Croy, Anita. *Jane Austen*. New York, NY: Lucent Press, 2020.

Lewis, Aura. *Spectacular Sisters: Amazing Stories of Sisters from Around the World*. New York, NY: Quill Tree Books, 2021.

Spinale, Laura. *Sojourner Truth: Abolitionist and Activist*. Mankato, MN: The Child's World, 2022.

WEBSITES

The Art Story: "Summary of Elisabeth Louise Vigée-Lebrun"
www.theartstory.org/artist/vigee-le-brun-elisabeth-louise
You can use this website to view many of Elisabeth Vigée-Lebrun's most famous paintings.

National Geographic Kids: "The Life of Florence Nightingale"
www.natgeokids.com/uk/discover/history/general-history/florence-nightingale
This article offers a look at Florence Nightingale's life and the important role she played in the history of nursing.

National Susan B. Anthony Museum and House
www.susanb.org
You can learn more about Susan B. Anthony's life and influence as a suffragist on this page.

Victoria and Albert Museum
www.vam.ac.uk/
Visit the website of the Victoria and Albert Museum in London to learn more about the museum that grew out of the Great Exhibition and that was opened by Queen Victoria herself.

INDEX

abolitionism, 25–26, 49–50, 52, 54
African Americans, 25, 50, 54
amendments, 49–50
American Civil War, 25, 27–28, 50, 54
artists, 6–7

Crimean War, 44, 56, 59

Declaration of Sentiments, 52
depression, 31, 41, 45
Disraeli, Benjamin, 45–47

education (of women), 7–9
England, 7, 10–11, 13–15, 19, 22, 27, 29–48, 55–59

feminism, 8, 35
France, 6, 9, 11, 12, 14
French Revolution, 6–7, 11, 14

Germany, 11, 13, 56
Great Exhibition, 43

hospitals, 28–29, 44, 47, 56, 58–60

imperialism, 46–48
India, 37, 46–47, 60
Ireland, 33, 37, 43, 46

Lewis and Clark Expedition, 22–25, 51

Marie-Antoinette, 6

memoirs, 6, 9, 10, 26
mental illness, 27–28
Mott, Lucretia, 25, 52

Napoleon, 6, 12–14, 21
novels, 7–9, 12, 14–22, 29–37, 43
nursing, 55–61

Ottoman Empire, 56

poetry, 10, 31–32, 36
prisons, 28

Quakers, 26, 49
queens, 6, 37–48, 59

Romanticism, 8–13, 18
Russia, 14, 46, 56

salons, 9–11, 14
satire, 18–21, 34–35
schools, 7, 27–31, 34–36, 49, 60
Shoshone, 22–25
slavery, 23, 25–27, 50, 52
South African War, 47
Switzerland, 6, 11, 13–14

teachers, 27, 30, 31, 35
temperance movement, 49, 54

United States, 22–29, 48–55

women's rights movement, 9, 25–27, 48–55
women's suffrage, 47–55
writers, 7–9, 9–15, 15–22, 29–37